# WOLFGANG AMADEUS MOZART

# FLUTE CONCERTO

D major/D-Dur/Ré majeur
K 314

## Ernst Eulenburg Ltd

London · Mainz · Madrid · New York · Paris · Prague · Tokyo · Toronto · Zürich

# CONTENTS

# PREFACE

Most of Mozart's soloistic and chamber music works for or with flute originated in the first half of 1778 in Mannheim and in Paris. He composed the two flute concertos K313 and 314, and the two flute quartets K285 and 28, for a rich Dutchman named Dejean (Dechamps) who ordered them in Mannheim in 1778 when he made his acquaintance. The concertos and the first quartet were completed not later than 14 February. The double concerto for flute and harp, K299, was written by Mozart for the Duc de Guines.[1] Work on these Mannheim compositions, to which the two concertos also count, did not flow easily. To his father he excused himself with the fact that he had such diverse obligations in Mannheim, and besides:

one is not at all times disposed to work. Of course I could jot down all day long: but a thing such as this goes out into the world, so it is my wish that I need not be ashamed that it carries my name. And then, as you know, I am always 'stuck' if I have to write all the time for one and the same instrument (which I dislike[2]) …

Nevertheless, at the age of twenty-two he created masterpieces within the scope of a highly cultured society music, masterpieces – and that holds good especially of the concertos which display to the best advantage the versatility and technique of the instrument, and give a perfect image of spirit and feeling of the rococo. In their general attitude, as in the overcoming of the formal problems, the concertos are actually close to the violin concertos of 1775, and even in a thematic respect many a turn, thus e. g. the beginning of both of the concertos, reveals the proximity of the violin concertos in D, B flat and G major. Surprising, therefore, are certain melodic ideas which we meet in full elaboration in the masterpieces of the 1780ies, but which are here suddenly anticipated. In this connection the 'bridging' thematic work deserves attention which leads glidingly into the theme to be intonated (K314, in the second theme and at the entry of the first solo).

Rudolf Gerber

Cp. Edition Eulenburg No. 767. On a third quartet cp.
H.Abert: *Mozart*, Vol.I, 596, footnote
Viz., the flute!

# VORWORT

Mozarts Solo- und Kammermusikwerke für Flöte bzw. mit Flötenbeteiligung entstanden im Wesentlichen in der ersten Hälfte des Jahres 1778 in Mannheim und in Paris. Die beiden Flötenkonzerte KV 313 und 314 und die beiden Flötenquartette KV 285 und 298 komponierte er im Auftrag eines reichen Holländers namens Dejean (Dechamps), der sie bei ihm im Dezember 1778 in Mannheim, wo er ihn kennenlernte, bestellte. Die Konzerte und das erste Quartett waren bis spätestens 14. Februar vollendet, während das zweite Quartett erst in Paris fertiggestellt wurde. Das Doppelkonzert für Flöte und Harfe KV 299 hat Mozart in Paris für den Herzog von Guines geschaffen.[1] Die Arbeit an den Mannheimer Werken, zu denen auch die beiden Konzerte gehören, ging ihm nicht leicht von der Hand. Seinem Vater gegenüber entschuldigt er sich damit, dass er in Mannheim so vielerlei Verpflichtungen habe, außerdem

zu allen Zeiten ist man auch nicht aufgelegt zur Arbeit. Hinschmieren könnte ich freylich den ganzen Tag fort: aber so eine Sache kommt in die Welt hinaus, und da will ich halt, dass ich mich nicht schämen darf, wenn mein Name darauf steht. Dann bin ich auch, wie sie wissen, gleich stuff, wenn ich immer, für ein Instrument (das ich nicht leiden kan[2]) schreiben soll …

Gleichwohl hat der 22-Jährige hier im Rahmen einer hochkultivierten Gesellschaftsmusik Meisterwerke geschaffen, die – und das gilt vor allem für die Konzerte – sowohl die Technik des Blasinstruments in vorzüglicher und allseitiger Weise zur Geltung kommen lassen, als auch Geist und Gemüt des Rokoko vollendet spiegeln. In der Gesamthaltung wie in der Bewältigung der formalen Probleme stehen die Konzerte durchaus den Violinkonzerten vom Jahre 1775 nahe, und auch in thematischer Hinsicht verrät manche Wendung, so z. B. der Anfang beider Konzerte, die Nachbarschaft der Violinkonzerte in D-, B- und G-Dur. Überraschend wirken deshalb auch manche melodische Gedanken, die in den großen Meisterwerken der 1780er Jahre in voller Ausformung entgegentreten, hier aber gleichsam blitzartig vorweggenommen werden. Beachtung verdient auch in diesem Zusammenhang die Erwähnung jener „Brückenthematik", durch die in das zu intonierende Thema hineingeglitten wird (KV 314 im 1. Satz beim 2. Thema und Eintritt des ersten Solos).

Rudolf Gerber

---

Vgl. Edition Eulenburg Nr. 767. Über ein drittes Quartett vgl. H. Abert, *Mozart*, Bd. 1, Seite 596, Anm.
Nämlich die Flöte!

# FLUTE CONCERTO

Wolfgang Amadeus Mozart
(1756–1791)
K 314

No. 771          EE 4894

2

3

4

6

7

9

10

12

15

16

II. Adagio ma non troppo

19

22

## III. RONDEAU

Allegro

26

28

32

36